To

From

For my little friend Isaac   A.W.

Written and compiled by Elena Pasquali
Illustrations copyright © 2016 Antonia Woodward
This edition copyright © 2016 Lion Hudson

The right of Antonia Woodward to be identified as the illustrator of this work has been asserted by her in accordance with the Copyright, Designs and Patents Act 1988.

All rights reserved. No part of this publication may be reproduced or transmitted in any form or by any means, electronic or mechanical, including photocopy, recording, or any information storage and retrieval system, without permission in writing from the publisher.

Published by Lion Children's Books
an imprint of
Lion Hudson plc
Wilkinson House, Jordan Hill Road,
Oxford OX2 8DR, England
www.lionhudson.com/lionchildrens

ISBN 978 0 7459 7628 0

First edition 2016

Author Information
p. 13: Julia Carney (1823–1908)
pp. 19, 34, 54: Sophie Piper
p. 21: From an old New England sampler
p. 25: John Chapman, planter of orchards (1774–1845)
pp. 26, 39: Cecil Frances Alexander (1818–95)
p. 28: Edith Rutter Leatham (1870–1939)
p. 52: John Leland (1754–1841)
p. 59: Christina Goodings

Acknowledgments
All unattributed prayers are by Elena Pasquali and Lois Rock, copyright © Lion Hudson.
Prayers by Sophie Piper and Christina Goodings are copyright © Lion Hudson.

Bible extracts are taken or adapted from the Good News Bible © 1994 published by the Bible Societies/HarperCollins Publishers Ltd UK, Good News Bible© American Bible Society 1966, 1971, 1976, 1992. Used with permission.

The Lord's Prayer (p. 46) as it appears in *Common Worship: Services and Prayers for the Church of England* (Church House Publishing, 2000) is copyright © The English Language Liturgical Consultation and is reproduced by permission of the publisher.

A catalogue record for this book is available from the British Library

Printed and bound in China, December 2015, LH25

The Lion Book of
NURSERY PRAYERS

Written and compiled by *Elena Pasquali*

Illustrated by *Antonia Woodward*

LION
CHILDREN'S

CONTENTS

BRIGHT NEW DAY 7
MORNING LIGHT 8
MY DAY BEGINS 10
BUSY, BUSY, BUSY 12
FINGER-COUNTING PRAYER 14

CIRCLE OF LOVE 17
MOTHER AND FATHER 18
MY FAMILY 20
AT HOME 22
TIME TO EAT 24

WONDERFUL WORLD 27
LITTLE CREATURES 28
AMAZING ANIMALS 30
CIRCLE OF LIFE 32

AROUND THE YEAR 35

CHRISTMAS 36

EASTER 38

HARVEST THANKSGIVING 40

GOD IN HEAVEN 43

HOORAY FOR GOD 44

OUR FATHER 46

THE GOOD SHEPHERD 48

BIBLE PRAYERS 50

GOODNIGHT, GOD BLESS 53

DAY IS DONE 54

NIGHT-TIME 56

TIME TO SLEEP 58

BLESSINGS 60

INDEX OF FIRST LINES 62

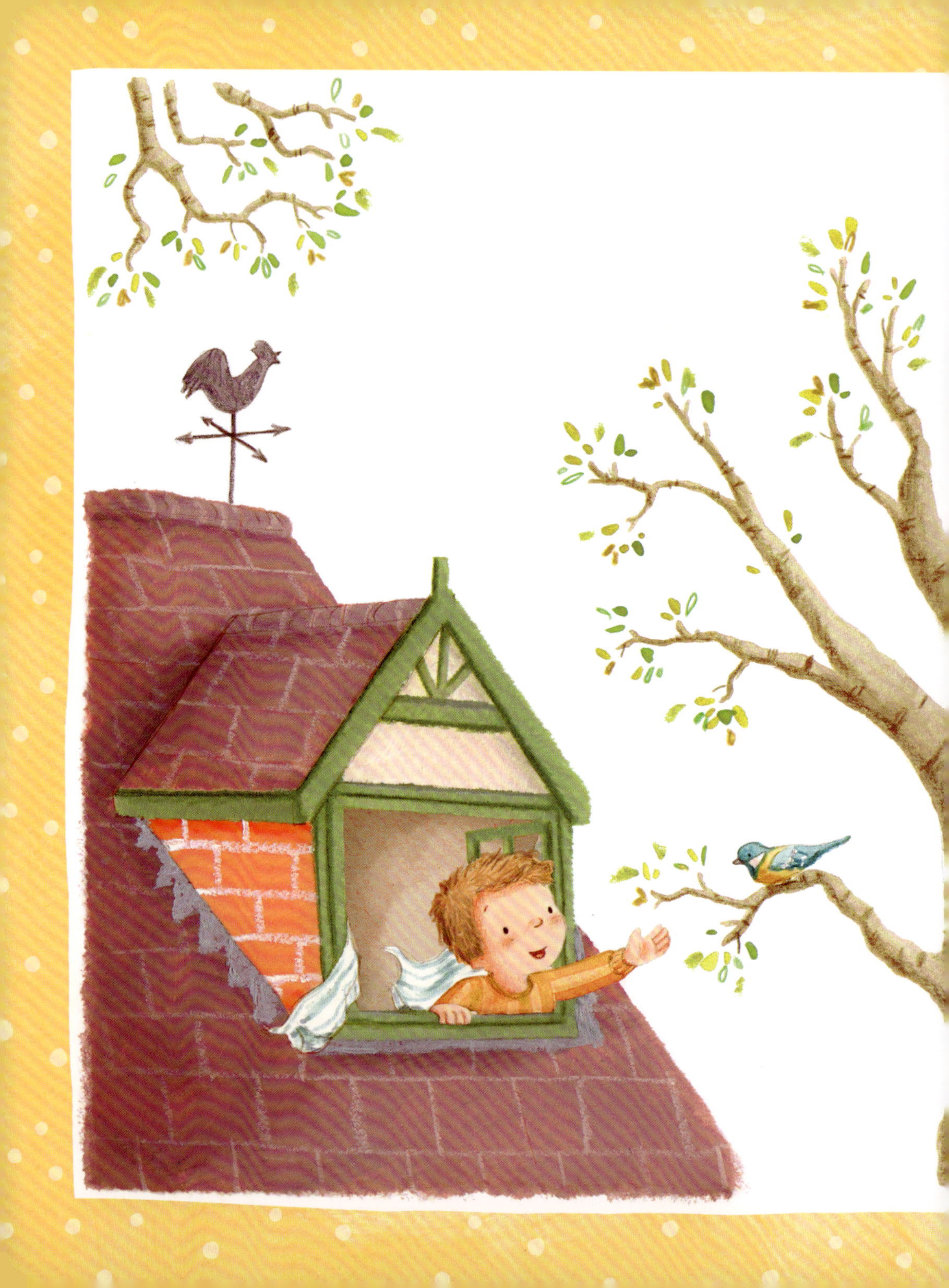

Bright New Day

Dearest God,
on this new day,
listen to me
as I pray.

Dearest God,
the day is new:
help me in
the things I do.

Morning Light

Quietly each morning,
I look up at the sky
To watch the dark grow paler
As sunrise lights the sky.
The day is all before me,
All fresh and bright and new,
And I ask God to guide me
In all I have to do.

I lift my hands to the golden sun:
A shining day has just begun.
I wave my hands to heaven above:
May God surround me with his love.

MY DAY BEGINS

I wake
I wash
I dress
I say:
"Thank you,
God,
for this
new day."

Bless my hair and bless my toes
Bless my ears and bless my nose
Bless my eyes and bless each hand
Bless the feet on which I stand
Bless my elbows, bless each knee:
God bless every part of me.

Busy, busy, busy

May my hands be helping hands
For all that must be done
That fetch and carry, lift and hold
And make the hard jobs fun.

May my hands be clever hands
In all I make and do
With sand and dough and clay and things
With paper, paint and glue.

May my hands be gentle hands
And may I never dare
To poke and prod and hurt and harm
But touch with love and care.

Little deeds of kindness,
Little words of love,
Help to make earth happy,
Like the heaven above.

TRADITIONAL

Finger-counting prayer

This is my prayer number 1:
bless the day that's just begun.
This is my prayer number 2:
may the sky be clear and blue.
This is my prayer number 3:
God, please take good care of me.
This is my prayer number 4:
help me love you more and more.
This is my prayer number 5:
make me glad to be alive.
This is my prayer number 6:
help me when I'm in a fix.
This is my prayer number 7:
make this world a bit like heaven.
This is my prayer number 8:
put an end to hurt and hate.
This is my prayer number 9:
let the light of kindness shine.
This is my prayer number 10:
bring me safe to bed again.

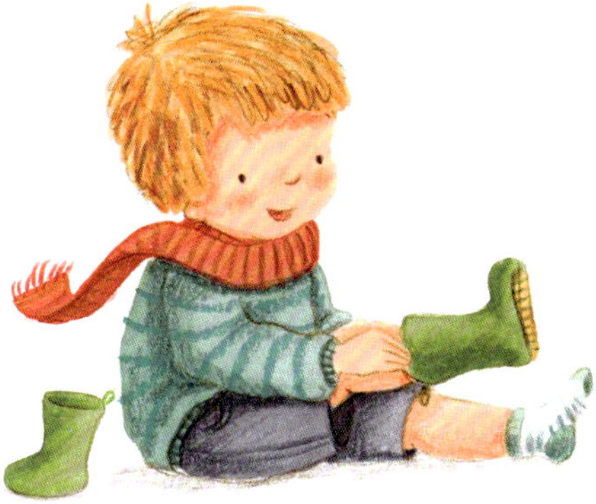

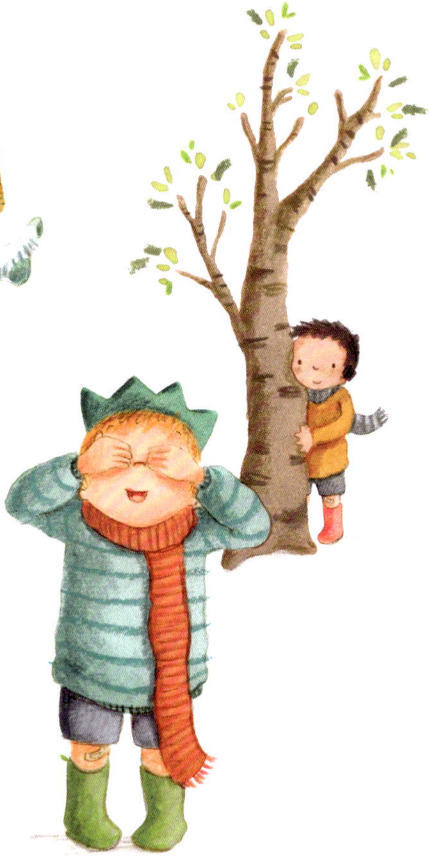

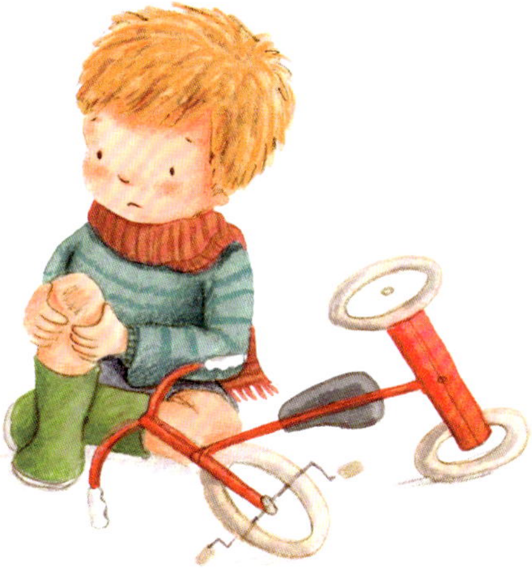

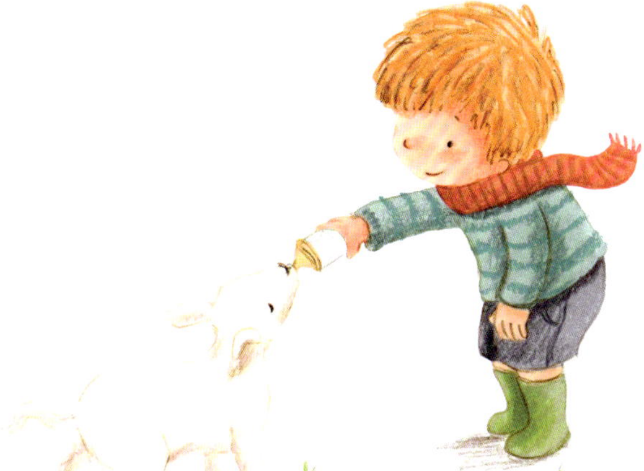

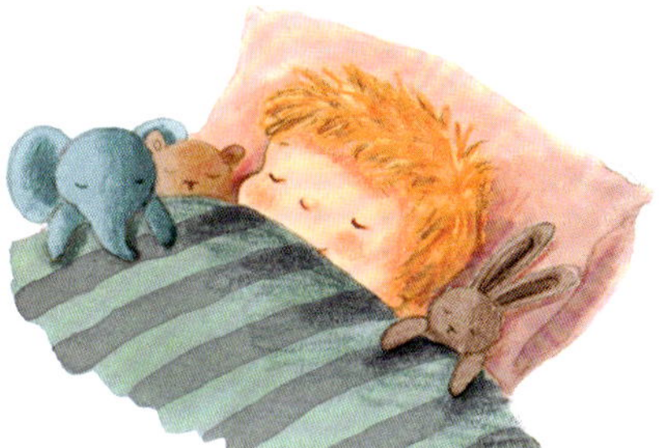

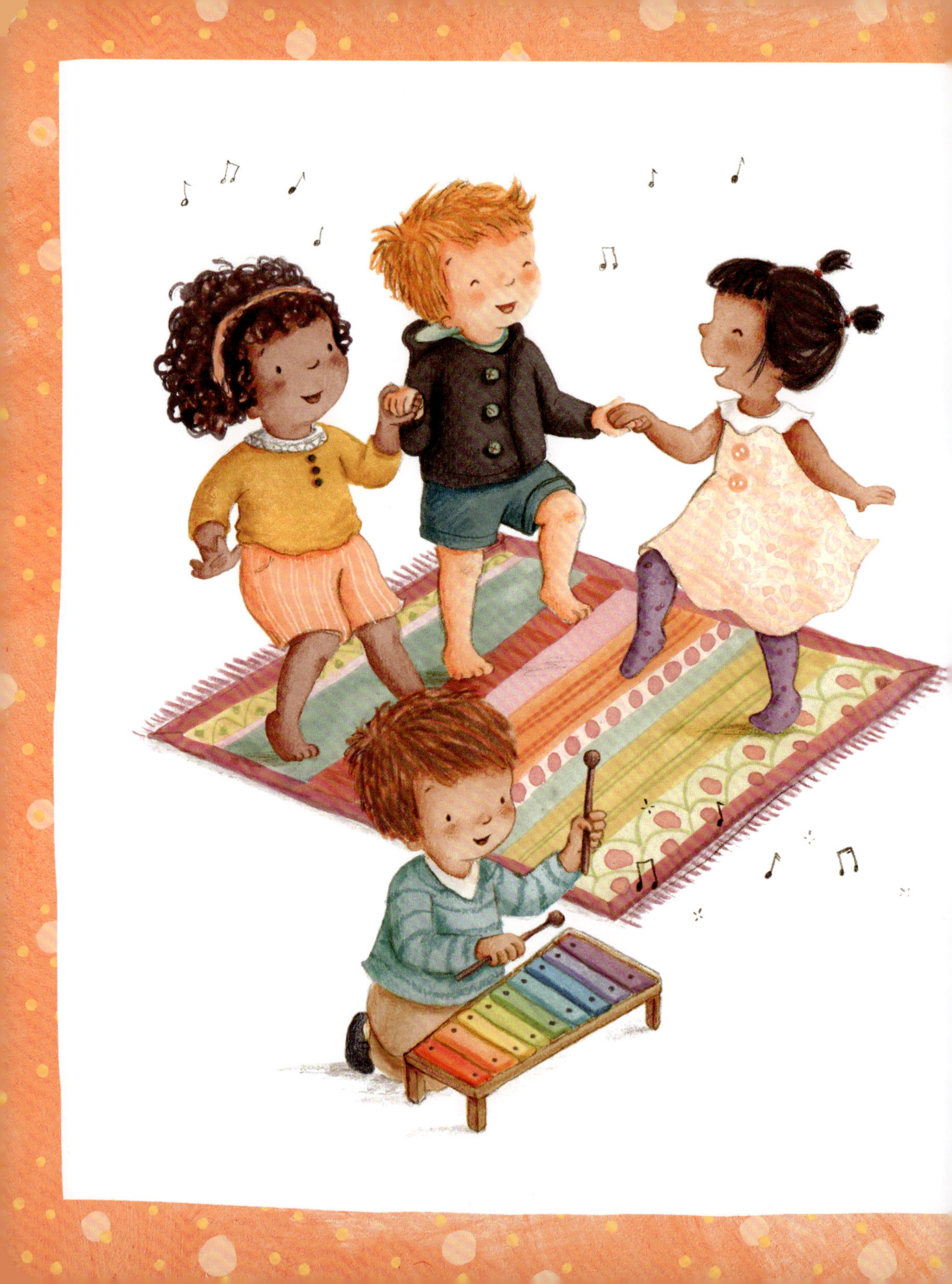

Circle of Love

Thank you, dear God,
for the many kind people
who help us along on our way,
who smile when we're glad
and who care when we're sad
and who keep us safe all through the day.

Mother and Father

Dear God, take care of Mother,
who takes good care of me,
and may our home be full of love
that all the world can see.

God bless my father
through the bright blue day.
God bless my father
through the starlit night.
God bless my father
when we hug together.
God bless my father
when he's out of sight.

*In both these prayers you can use the special name
you have for your mother and father.*

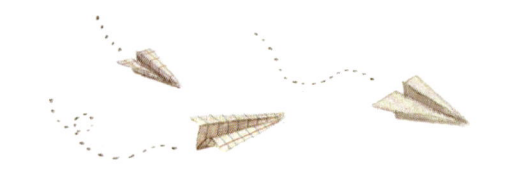

My family

Dear God, bless all my family,
as I tell you each name;
and please bless each one differently
for no one's quite the same.

God bless all those that I love;
God bless all those that love me;
God bless all those that love those that I love,
And all those that love those that love me.

TRADITIONAL

At home

Bless the window
Bless the door
Bless the ceiling
Bless the floor
Bless this place
which is our home
Bless us as we go
and come.

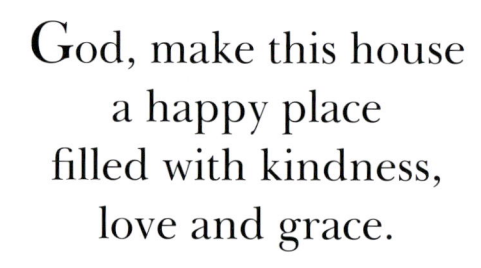

God, make this house
a happy place
filled with kindness,
love and grace.

Bless the mess
but make us strong
to put things
where they belong.

May our home be full of love
May our home be bright
Filled with laughter through the day
And full of peace at night.

Time to eat

Let us take a moment
To thank God for our food
For friends around the table
And everything that's good.

The Lord is good to me,
And so I thank the Lord
For giving me the things I need,
The sun, the rain, the appleseed.
The Lord is good to me.

TRADITIONAL

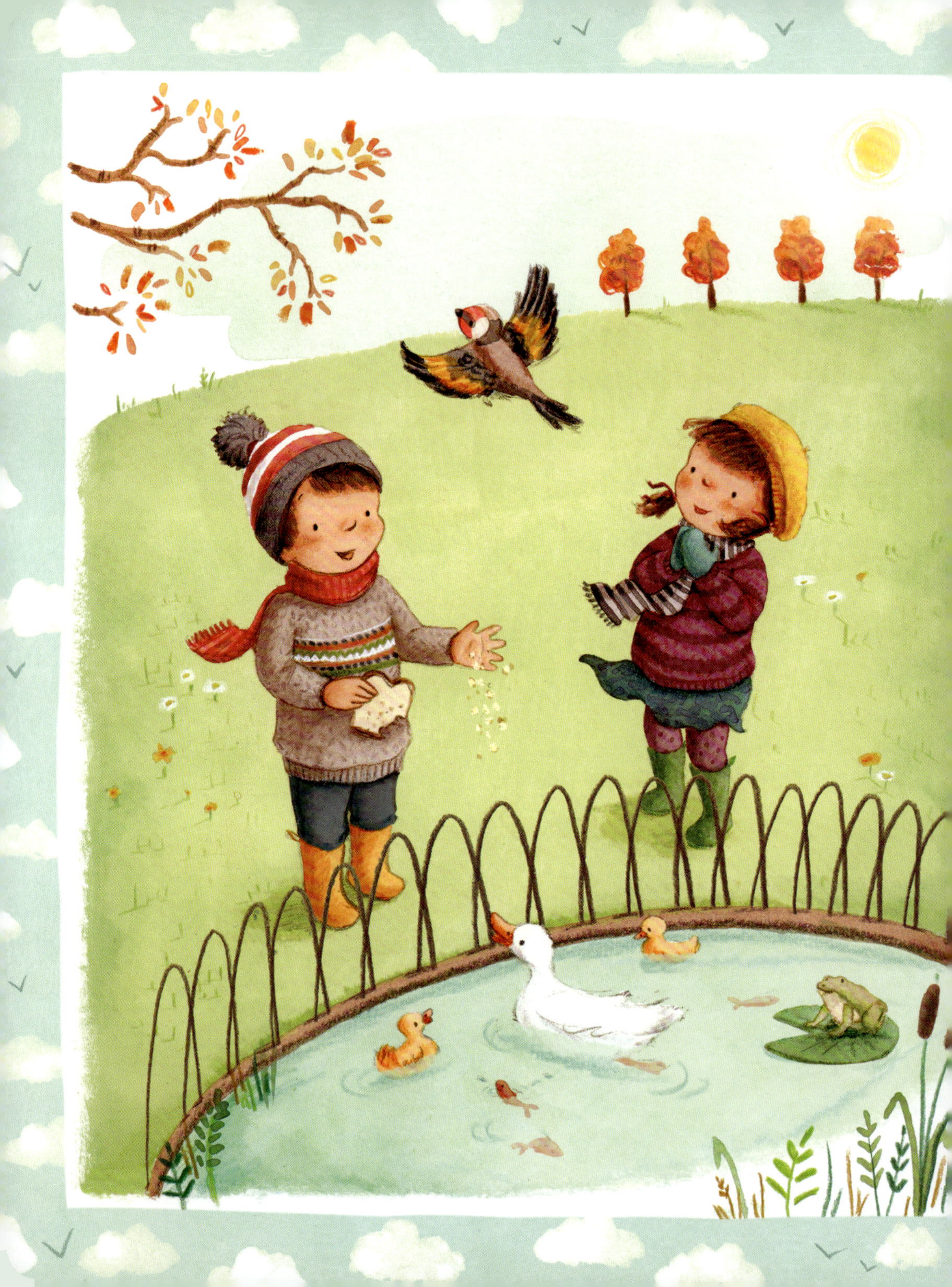

Wonderful World

All things bright and beautiful,
All creatures great and small,
All things wise and wonderful,
The Lord God made them all.

A CHILDREN'S HYMN

LITTLE CREATURES

Dear Father, hear and bless
your beasts and singing birds,
and guard with tenderness
small things that have no words.

TRADITIONAL

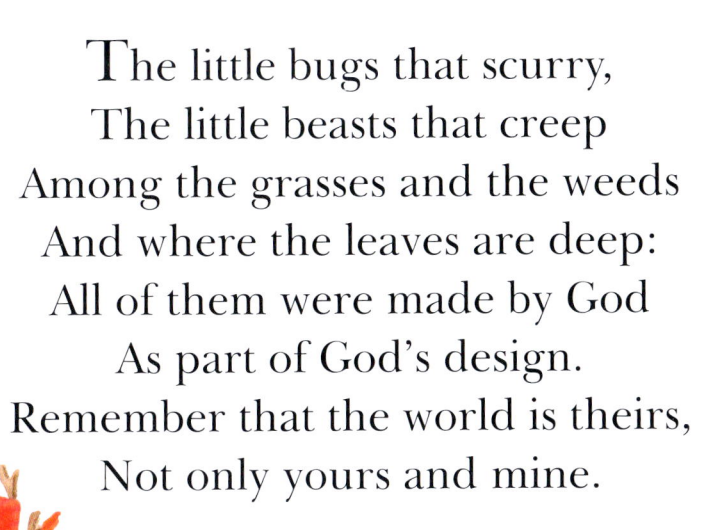

The little bugs that scurry,
The little beasts that creep
Among the grasses and the weeds
And where the leaves are deep:
All of them were made by God
As part of God's design.
Remember that the world is theirs,
Not only yours and mine.

Amazing animals

Bless the hungry lion and its ROAR
Bless the big brown bear and its GROWL
Bless the sly hyena and its scary HA HA HA
Bless the wolves who see the moon and HOWL!

Multicoloured animals
With stripes and dots and patches:
God made each one different –
There isn't one that matches.

Circle of Life

Baby creatures, just awakened,
You are part of God's creation;
Baby creatures, oh, so small,
God is father of us all.

When little creatures die
And it's time to say goodbye
To a bright-eyed furry friend,
We know that God above
Will remember them with love:
A love that will never end.

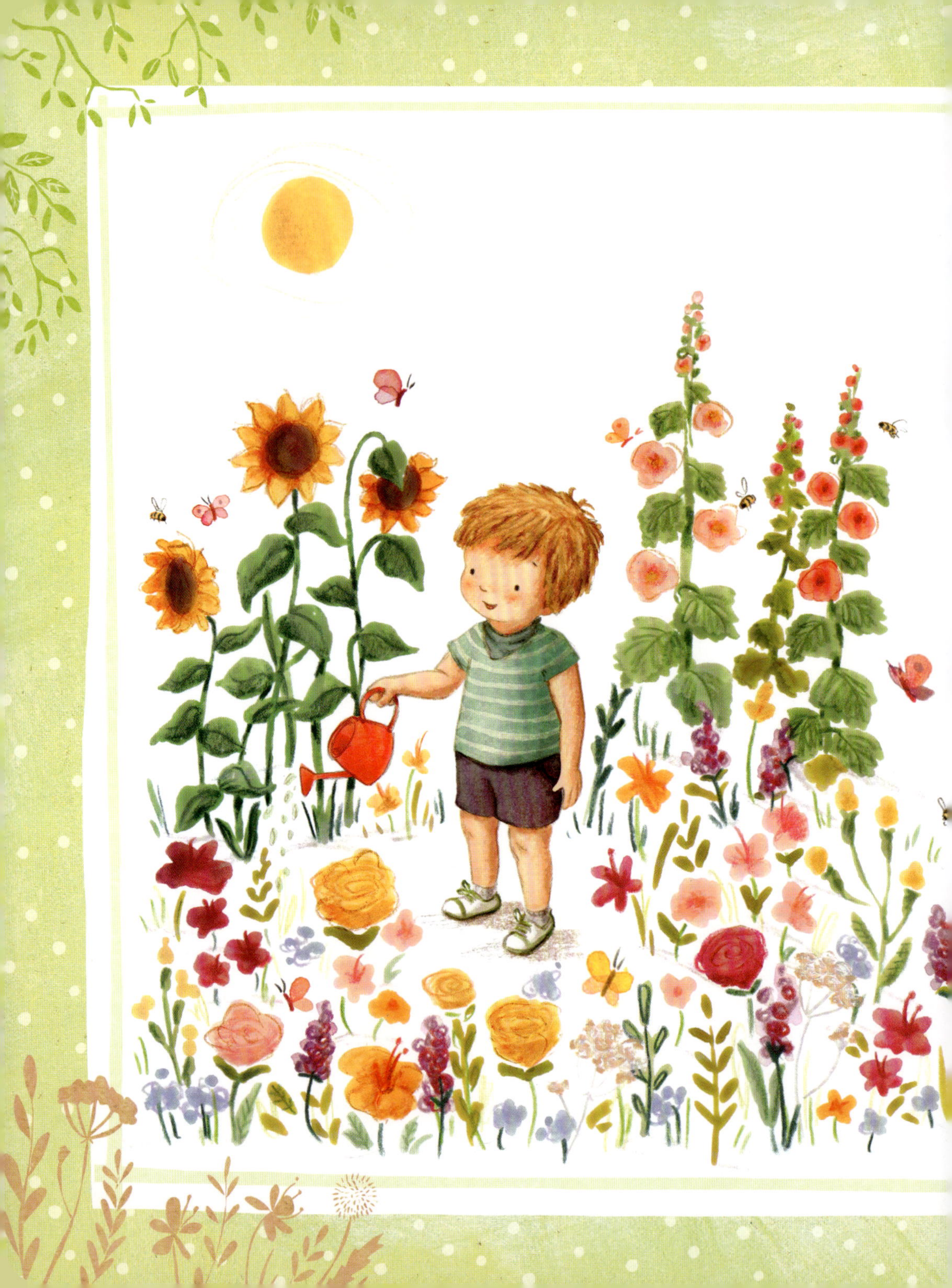

Around the Year

Thank you for spring
and the waking time.

Thank you for summer
and the growing time.

Thank you for autumn
and the gathering time.

Thank you for winter
and the resting time.

CHRISTMAS

Let us travel to Christmas
By the light of a star.
Let us go to the hillside
Right where the shepherds are.
Let us see shining angels
Singing from heaven above.
Let us see Mary and Jesus –
Who brings us God's heavenly love.

I am little
I am lowly
God is great and
God is holy;

yet was born
a child like me
here on earth
for all to see;

came from heaven –
great and holy –
to a stable:
little, lowly.

Easter

In the Easter garden
the leaves are turning green;
in the Easter garden
the risen Christ is seen.

In the Easter garden
we know that God above
brings us all to heaven
through Jesus and his love.

There is a green hill far away,
Outside a city wall,
Where the dear Lord was crucified
Who died to save us all.

He died that we might be forgiven,
He died to make us good;
That we might go at last to heaven,
Saved by his precious blood.

A CHILDREN'S HYMN

Harvest thanksgiving

The harvest of our garden
is astonishingly small;
but oh, dear God, we thank you
that there's anything at all.

Seed and shoot and ear and grain
Growing in the sun and rain.
Grain and flour and dough and bread –
By God's harvest we are fed.

We plough the land,
God sends the rain
to bring the harvest
once again;
and when the fields
of wheat turn gold,
then God's great goodness
must be told.

BASED ON PSALM 65

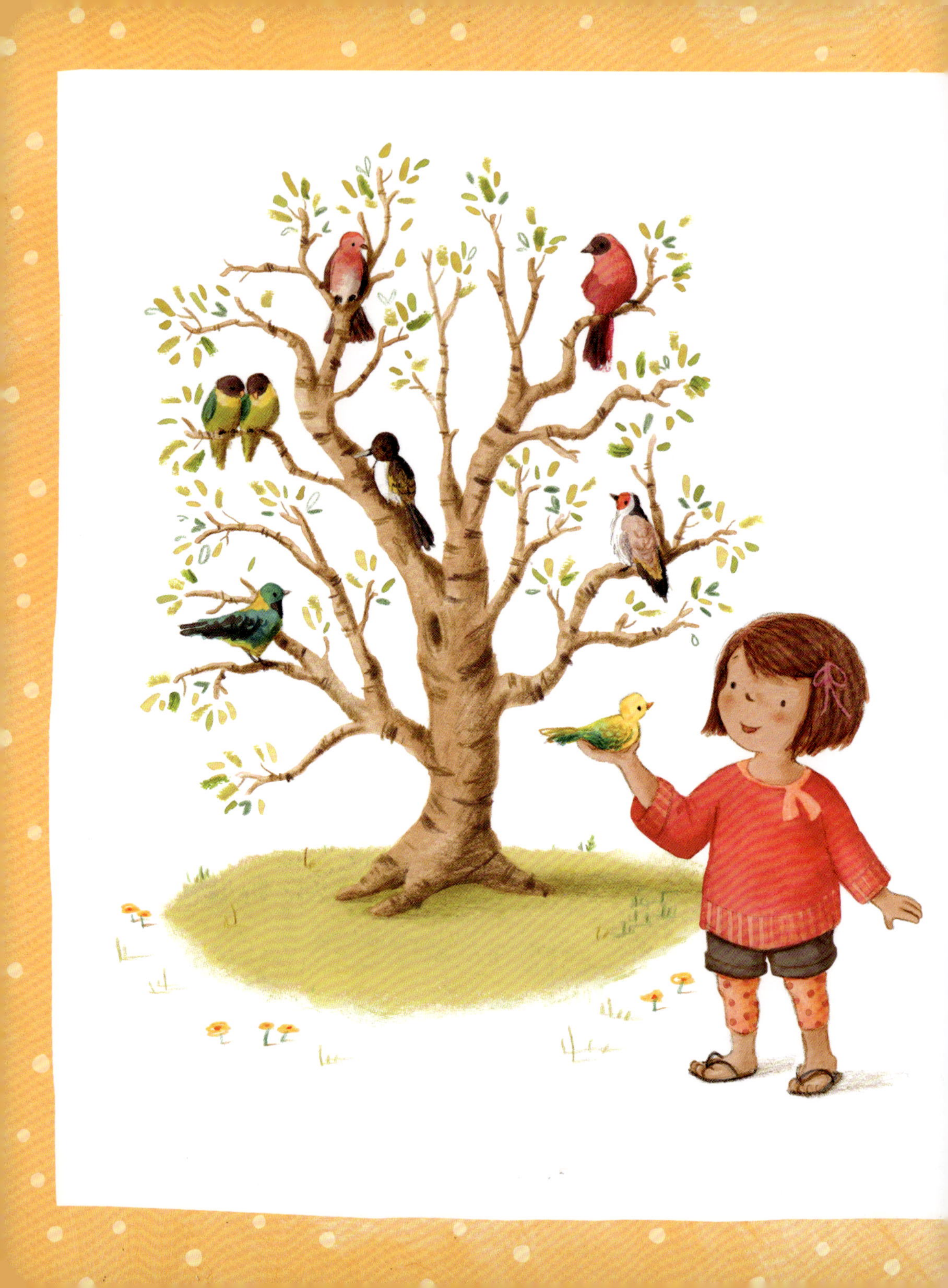

God in Heaven

God, look down from heaven:
Here on earth you'll see
Someone looking upwards –
That someone is me.

Hooray for God

Sing to God with thankfulness,
sing a song of praise,
sing out loud and joyfully,
sing out all your days.

FROM PSALM 95

Praise God on the noisy drum
Rumpty tumpty tumpty tum.

Praise God with a mighty clash
Let the cymbals crash-a-bash.

Praise God on the gentle flute
Tootle tootle tootle toot.

Praise God as you pluck the strings
Tring a ling a ling a ling.

Play the trumpet, rum pah pah
May your praises sound afar.

FROM PSALM 150

Our Father

Jesus gave his followers a prayer to say:

Our Father in heaven,
hallowed be your name,
your kingdom come,
your will be done,
on earth as in heaven.
Give us today our daily bread.
Forgive us our sins
as we forgive those who sin against us.
Lead us not into temptation
but deliver us from evil.

FROM MATTHEW 6 AND LUKE 11

For hundreds of years, people have often added this ending:

For the kingdom, the power,
and the glory are yours
now and for ever.
Amen

The Good Shepherd

Dear God, you are my shepherd,
You give me all I need,
You take me where the grass grows green
And I can safely feed.

You take me where the water
Is calm and cool and clear;
And there I rest and know I'm safe
For you are always near.

BASED ON PSALM 23

Dear God,
I am your lost sheep.
I stopped listening to your voice.
I did not obey what you told me.
Now I feel sad and alone.
Please come and find me.
Please welcome me home.
Please make me glad again.

BASED ON JESUS' PARABLE OF THE LOST SHEEP

Bible prayers

I will choose the narrow path,
I will walk the straight,
Through the wide and winding world
Up to heaven's gate.

BASED ON MATTHEW 7

I've taken off the old me
and thrown it all away;
I'm going to be the new me
as from this very day.

BASED ON COLOSSIANS 3

May my life shine
like a star in the night,
filling my world
with goodness and light.

FROM PHILIPPIANS 2

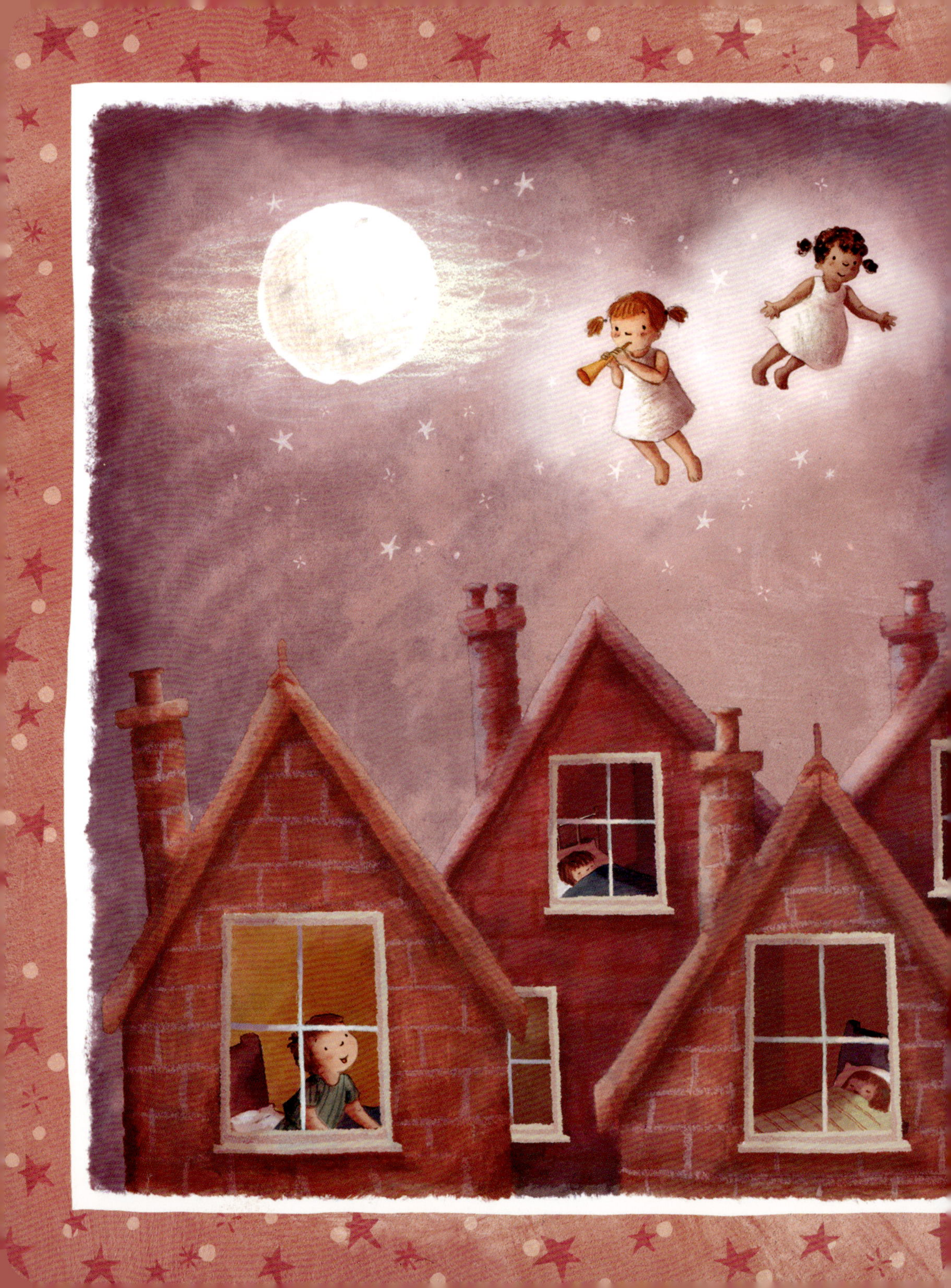

Goodnight, God Bless

Lord, keep us safe this night,
Secure from all our fears;
May angels guard us while we sleep,
Till morning light appears.

TRADITIONAL

Day is done

The darkness comes:
Give thanks for the night.

The stars appear:
Give thanks for their light.

The air is still:
Give thanks for the calm.

And God is here:
Keep us safe from harm.

I see the moon
And the moon sees me;
God bless the moon
And God bless me.

TRADITIONAL

Night-time

Day is done,
Gone the sun
From the lake,
From the hills,
From the sky.
Safely rest,
All is well!
God is nigh.

ANONYMOUS

God bless the night-time creatures
in the shadows of the wood;
may they live their secret lives
as wild creatures should.

May they find their secret paths
through all the moonlit dark;
may they find their secret homes
when morning wakes the lark.

Time to sleep

Now I lay me down to sleep,
I pray thee, Lord, thy child to keep;
Thy love to guard me through the night
And wake me in the morning light.

TRADITIONAL

When I lie down, I go to sleep in peace;
you alone, O Lord, keep me perfectly safe.

PSALM 4:8

Blessings

Deep peace of the running waves to you,
Deep peace of the flowing air to you,
Deep peace of the quiet earth to you,
Deep peace of the shining stars to you,
Deep peace of the shades of night to you,
Moon and stars always giving light to you,
Deep peace of Christ, the Son of Peace, to you.

TRADITIONAL GAELIC BLESSING

Clouds in the sky above,
Waves on the sea,
Angels up in heaven
Watching over you and me.

Index of First Lines

All things bright and beautiful   27
Baby creatures, just awakened   32
Bless my hair and bless my toes   11
Bless the hungry lion and its ROAR   30
Bless the mess   23
Bless the window   22
Clouds in the sky above   61
Day is done   56
Dear Father, hear and bless   28
Dear God, bless all my family   20
Dear God, I am your lost sheep   49
Dear God, take care of Mother   18
Dear God, you are my shepherd   48
Dearest God, on this new day   7
Deep peace of the running waves to you   60
God bless all those that I love   21
God bless my father   19
God bless the night-time creatures   57
God has counted the stars in the heavens 64
God, look down from heaven   43
God, make this house   22
I am little   37
I lift my hands to the golden sun   9
I see the moon   55
I wake   10

I will choose the narrow path	50
I've taken off the old me	50
In the Easter garden	38
Let us take a moment	24
Let us travel to Christmas	36
Little deeds of kindness	13
Lord, keep us safe this night	53
May my hands be helping hands	12
May my life shine	51
May our home be full of love	23
Multicoloured animals	31
Now I lay me down to sleep	58
Our Father in heaven	46
Praise God on the noisy drum	45
Quietly each morning	8
Seed and shoot and ear and grain	41
Sing to God with thankfulness	44
Thank you, dear God, for the many kind people	17
Thank you for spring	35
The darkness comes	54
The harvest of our garden	40
The little bugs that scurry	29
The Lord is good to me	25
There is a green hill far away	39
This is my prayer number 1	14
We plough the land	41
When I lie down, I go to sleep in peace	59
When little creatures die	33

God has counted the stars in the heavens,
God has counted the leaves on the tree;
God has counted the children on earth:
I know God has counted me.